ASK *
YOUR
MOTHER

By Ruth Carpenter

* Just add some common sense

First published in Great Britain in 2005 by Robson
Books, The Chrysalis Building, Bramley Road, London
W10 6SP

An imprint of Chrysalis Books Group plc

First published in 2004 by Gusto Company AS
Copyright © 2004, 2005 Gusto Company AS

British Library Cataloguing in Publication Data
A catalogue for this title is available from the
British Library

1 86105 861 6

Original concept by James Tavendale and
Ernesto Gremese
Illustrated by Greg Paprocki, Artville and Photodisc
Original design by Bulle Visjon
Original cover design by SEE Design
Printed by SNP Leefung, China

Fifty Things

Your Mother Should

Have Taught You

But Probably Didn't

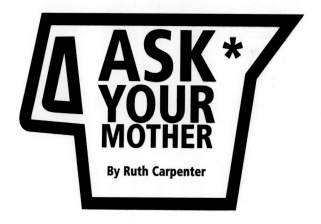

ASK *
YOUR
MOTHER

By Ruth Carpenter

* Just add some common sense

INTRODUCTION

Much is made of a girl's relationship with her mother. Whether you're best friends or fight like cat and dog, there's an unspoken bond that is the mother daughter thing.

. . . .

Your mother is there at all the milestones that make up your life – from girlhood to womanhood. She will comfort you when you fight with your best friend at school, help you with the uncertain feelings and embarrassment of your teens and becoming a woman, sympathise when your boyfriend dumps you and help you to plan your wedding.

But what about the things she didn't teach you? Does your mum know any self defence? And would you really want to talk to her about sex tips that men love? Can she conduct a networking lunch or do a striptease? Perhaps you'd rather not know that last one.

I have a great relationship with my own mum and take it as a compliment when told by people that I take after her. But I wouldn't want her on my hen night or like her to advise me on my sex life. And even though she probably knows how to set a dinner table correctly or pack for a long weekend, she's never sat down and taught me.

So to supplement the maternal curriculum, *Ask Your Mother* will give you an insight into fifty things that your mother may or may not know but didn't teach you.

They'll help you to boost your knowledge and increase your life experience. And who knows? You might be able to teach your mother something.

Ruth Carpenter

CONTENTS

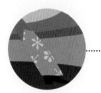

CHAPTER 3 / Baking, homemaking and being a domestic goddess

CHAPTER 4 / How to be 'all woman'

CHAPTER 1

Style
AND ETIQUETTE

Apply Lipstick
Correctly

How you apply your lipstick and which colour you choose depends a lot on the look you are going for.
....

A natural look can get away with less than perfect application. But for lips that look great and lipstick that stays put there are a few rules you should follow. Firstly, get your lips in condition by buffing gently with a lip scuff, toothbrush or face cloth to remove any unattractive, dry or flaky skin.

For super smooth smackers, moisturise your lips with a lip balm. Avoid medicated ones and really greasy balms as these don't make a good base for your lipstick.

With a strong colour lipstick, like red, apply it directly from the tube onto your bottom lip. Then put your lips together and fill in the rest of your mouth using a lip brush.

Make your lipstick last by applying lots of thin layers with a lip brush and working it into your lips. Blot with a tissue to absorb the oil in the product and leave the pigment; then apply a last layer of colour.

Forget lip liner – so dated – filling in colour using a lip brush gives a softer more wearable finish. If you must use lip liner, use a colour a shade lighter than your lipstick and blend it in so you don't leave a harsh outline. The object is to stop your lipstick bleeding, not to look like a clown!

If you have very thin lips then it's best to avoid deep colours like red, as they'll make your mouth look even smaller. Try red or berry gloss for a fuller pout.

If you go for the less is more approach – pale, nude tones – white teeth are a must. Invest in some whitening toothpaste and avoid coffee, tea and red wine, which can stain teeth.

If you like bright or bold tones but haven't quite got the courage to wear them on your lips, try a gloss instead. Because they are transparent you can go for a strong colour you wouldn't normally dare with a lipstick.

Eating and drinking can easily remove lipstick – try lightly licking your lips before drinking to stop lipstick transferring to a glass or cup. And always carry a pocket mirror in your handbag so you can re-apply.

Finally, pucker up, those lips look good enough to kiss!

Avoid Fashion
Faux Pas

Being fashionable and looking good are not the same thing. We all want to keep up with what's current but sometimes need a little help to keep it on track.

Advice like this should be given to you by your mother with the same importance as the birds and the bees – she did tell you about that didn't she?

If in doubt go classic

An indispensable piece of advice – if you're not sure what's in and what's not, look to buy classic items of clothing. A classic pair of Levis, white shirt, black polo neck, trench coat, pencil skirt, straight-leg black trousers are all items that will never date.

Use a personal shopper

This will enable you to use your time efficiently, buy things that suit you and work to a budget. The personal shopper's job is to have an overview of current trends leaving you stylish and not a bad case for the fashion cops.

Less is more

Streamlining your wardrobe is the first step to looking good. It's scary but few things are as satisfying as bringing order to a closet in which chaos has reigned.

Your personal style will begin to flourish once you realise that you really don't need as much clothing, accessories, jewellery or make-up as you once thought you did. Less is definitely more.

Think about the different looks you need for your lifestyle – corporate, casual, out with friends, cocktail party – and group clothes accordingly. Then try grouping clothes according to colour and you may create an outfit you didn't know existed.

Get a friend to come round while you try things on. She must be brutally honest – the aim is to get rid of things you don't need.

SHOP CAREFULLY

Be sensible. If neon is the hottest new trend and you simply must wear it, do so in small doses. For trends that won't last, a watch strap, a belt or bag will capture the look yet won't break the bank.

Investing in good-quality basics and updating with a few accessories every year will keep you looking stylish not freakish.

Above all, never fall into the following categories:

◇ Mutton dressed as lamb
◇ Letting it all hang out
◇ Prostitute chic
◇ Fifties headmistress

Buy a Capsule Wardrobe

The theory is that you should have some wardrobe basics that will stand the test of time and can be combined to take you through most situations – work, weekend and evening.

This is easier said than done. Your mother may have given you some advice about how to dress but unless she's an innately stylish woman whose dress sense provokes envy wherever she goes (there aren't many like her around), chances are you'll need some pointers. Here are some ground rules to get you started.

Age, Shape, Style

Any rules on how to dress stylishly will be tempered by the following three things: age, shape and personal style.

Age – isn't it hard when time decrees you should dress differently to the way you feel? Luckily, fashion is much more flexible these days so don't panic too much. Just remember to simplify things as you get older. Teenagers and twenty-somethings can get away with wearing different trends, colours and accessories at once but calm it down as you get older for a truly stylish look.

Shape – be realistic – whatever your shape, not everything is going to suit you.

Big boobs should avoid chunky knits, horizontal stripes and boxy or double-breasted jackets. Go for fine knit deep V-necks or wrap cardigans and get your bra professionally fitted.

Pear shapes need to steer clear of tapered and cropped trousers, anything cut on the bias and shapeless, baggy tops that will make the waist vanish. Try A-line skirts, flares or bootleg trousers, three-quarter length jackets and wear dark colours on the lower half.

Slim and boyish shapes should avoid the skinny bean look. Don't wear straight-legged hipsters or anything that emphasises your lack of bust, such as wrap tops and corsets, shift dresses and double-breasted styles. Go for A-line skirts, halter necks, simple style jumpers, shirts with front detail and hip hugging flared jeans.

Personal style – we don't all want to look the same but equally we don't want to look a mess. Think hard about the things you like. Is there a skirt length, colour or jacket shape that's you? If so, own this style and make it your signature.

It is best if this signature is something classic like a trench coat, bomber jacket, fitted shirt or straight skirt. You can update the colour, fabric or details, but keep the core components the same so you have a definable style.

BASICS
Things all women should have in their wardrobe:

Jeans – two pairs, one for 'dressy', one for casual. Go for current styles that will keep your look up-to-date

Suit – a trouser suit with matching skirt. You can mix and match, dress it up or down. Ideally go for classic tailoring and colours

White shirt – slightly fitted is great, again this can be dressed up for work or worn with jeans for a more casual look

Classic knits – don't let this make you think you have to look like your granny. A couple of plain, light knit sweaters (V-neck or crew neck) can be accessorised to complement any look

Leather jacket – style-wise it's up to you but, classic or contemporary, a leather jacket adds a bit of rebel to your basics

Plain Tees – plain fitted T-shirts will never let you down and are easily replaced when needed

Shoes – long boots to be worn with skirts, a pair of smart comfy flats, up-to-date trainers, classic heels and strappy sandals should see you through most situations

TIPS
◊ Get an appointment with a personal shopper for a completely objective view

◊ To stand out look for more interesting tops. Keep to classic shapes, but find interesting colours and textures or details to add interest

◊ Consider buying some shirts with Lycra™ which travel better than pure cotton

◊ Accessorise, accessorise, accessorise! Make any look in your capsule wardrobe fabulous with up-to-the-minute accessories

CHOOSING AND WEARING PERFUME

Your perfume is a way of expressing your personality and adds a finishing touch to what you're wearing. It is easy to be persuaded by the image of a perfume created by advertising, but it is a mistake to decide what suits you without trying a perfume out properly.

....

The first step is to think about what kinds of smells you find most attractive. Do you love the smell of a cake baking? Or does the smell of roses do it for you? Maybe you like the smell of the sea or fresh laundry, or perhaps the mossy scent of the woods.

Deciding on the type of smells you like will help you when deciding on a perfume, as fragrances generally fall into four main groups:

FLORAL
Like the name of this group suggests, flower scents are dominant in these perfumes. You'll like them if you're an optimist by nature and enjoy uncomplicated, beautiful scents.
Classic scent: Chanel No.5

Fresh

Clean, simple and contemporary, these fragrances are great for daytime wear or for those who hate a 'heavy' perfume. If you tend to think wearing perfume is not for you, you might actually find you like fresh fragrances.
Classic scent: CKOne

Chypre

These woody perfumes are heady and distinctive. In this family oak moss, bergamot, jasmine, rose, spice or wood scents are commonly used. You'll like them if you're a work hard, play hard type who goes for understated elegance.
Classic scent: Miss Dior

Oriental

This is by far the sexiest fragrance family, with perfumes containing ingredients such as vanilla and sandalwood. If you like this group you'll be a sensualist who knows how to use your femininity to your advantage.
Classic scent: Coco by Chanel

Tips

◊ When you buy a perfume, always try it out on your skin, not on the little bits of cardboard you're offered at the perfume counter. Perfume mixes with your own personal scent and smell and is different on different people. Never assume that a perfume that smells great on a friend will smell good on you

◊ Don't sniff the perfume immediately after you spray it. Remember that most perfumes contain three layers called top, middle and base notes. You cannot judge a perfume simply on its top notes, although this is what will make the first

impression. Leave it for an hour or so and then smell again to get the full impact of the fragrance. It is the base notes of a perfume that determine its fragrance family

◊ The difference between Eau de Toilette and Eau de Parfum is the concentration of the fragrance. The Eau de Parfum has a higher concentration of scent than the Eau de Toilette, meaning the perfume's scent will last longer on your skin

◊ Perfume will last about four hours before you need to re-apply and to ensure the scent lasts you should apply it strategically at different points of your body

◊ Oily skin holds a scent much longer than dry skin so those with dry skin will need to re-apply perfume more often

◊ On average a perfume should last about six months and should be kept in a cool dark place

DON'T GO TO YOUR BOSS
WITH A PROBLEM IF YOU
HAVEN'T SPENT AT LEAST
TEN MINUTES THINKING OF
POSSIBLE SOLUTIONS.

GET ON WITH YOUR BOSS

We're not talking about making your boss your best friend. Here are a few tips that will help ease your way in the workplace and – who knows? – may even get you a promotion...

....

There are several sure-fire ways you can make your working relationship more profitable, even if you have the boss from hell.

DON'T ASK QUESTIONS YOU CAN ANSWER

It's all too easy to ask your boss when you're not sure how to do something or want their approval. But next time, ask yourself: 'Will they be able to solve this problem any better than I can?' In most cases, probably not. You know your job better than anyone else so be resourceful and think things through first.

SOLUTIONS, NOT PROBLEMS

Don't go to your boss with a problem if you haven't spent at least ten minutes thinking of possible solutions. It will impress your boss if you go to him/her with a tricky issue and then suggest ways to resolve it.

DON'T GET EMOTIONAL

Don't ever send an email or confront your boss in a moment of anger or frustration. It's tempting to wade right in and say what's on your mind.

ULTIMATELY WORK IS WORK. YOU SHOULDN'T EXPECT TO SOCIALISE WITH YOUR BOSS OR KNOW THE INTIMATE DETAILS ABOUT THEIR PERSONAL LIFE.

Instead, write down your response to the situation. Wait at least half an hour, then think about what made you angry and read your written response to it. Nine times out of ten, you will have calmed down and can offer a much more constructive and considered response. Your boss will admire your diplomacy.

Go beyond the call of duty

Take on new challenges. Sometimes, the best way to find your calling is by trying new things. You may well learn something new and your boss will be impressed by your team spirit and remember that you pitched in to help.

Don't insult their intelligence

Sending an email, text message or calling in sick to a colleague is a sure sign that you're lying. Grow up and call your boss directly.

Ask for and give feedback

Communication works both ways and we all respond well to positive feedback. If there's something that your boss does that you like, tell them. Simply saying, 'I appreciated your support in that meeting' will highlight how their actions affect you. Positive feedback will reinforce the behaviour and will improve your working relationship.

Be proactive

We all have lots of suggestions on how to improve things at work or ideas for new projects. It's no use just sending your boss a list of ideas. Pick one or two of the best ideas and follow them through. Your boss will not only admire your innovative thinking, but the initiative you've taken to make them happen.

Realise your boss is not your friend

He or she may be a great person. But ultimately work is work. You shouldn't expect to socialise with your boss or know the intimate details about their personal life. Respecting your boss and working on friendly terms is much more important than them being the life and soul of the office party.

How to Buy
Underwear

It should be every mother's duty to inform her daughter about the great journey south.

....

That's when childbirth, age and too many glasses of Chardonnay take their toll and a woman's body starts letting gravity get the upper hand. Breasts, stomachs and bottoms journey downwards.

This is fatal and unless you have the money (and the nerve) to consider the drastic option of surgery, all you need to know is that good underwear is a girl's best friend.

But while underwear can make you look good in clothes you shouldn't expect miracles. It's not structural engineering.

Firstly you need to examine where you buy your underwear. 'Down the market' just isn't going to work if you want the illusion of a splendid physique. And as apparently three quarters of us girls are wearing the wrong size bra, getting property fitted is the essential place to start.

Most big department stores have a bra fitting service, as do specialist lingerie shops. So go and get measured! For the very peak of bra-fitting (no pun intended) you could do worse than try Rigby & Peller, suppliers of underwear to Her Majesty the Queen.

Underwear for the lower half is trickier but not impossible. Remember you want to create smooth lines under your clothes not ridges, lumps and bumps. Be honest about the size of your bottom half. Knickers that are too tight are uncomfortable and unsightly and who wants to look like they've been wrapped in electric cable when they take their clothes off?

If wearing a fitted pencil skirt or clinging dress, you could try a control girdle to create smooth lines around the lower half. A girdle may conjure up images of your granny but today's hi-tech fabrics mean that girdles are much more effective than they used to be and a lot easier on the eye.

After following these basic rules here's some advice to consider when buying underwear:

For small busts

The natural inclination is to wear a padded bra to increase bust size. However, they often leave empty space at the top of the bra where the straps start, which creates nasty ridges under clothes. Far better is to use silicone gel inserts that give a natural feel and fill out the bra. Place the gel insert beneath the breast so that you get a fuller, rounded shape. This works especially well if you try it while wearing an under-wired bra.

For big boobs

Bigger-breasted women often spill out of their bras, making it seem as if they have four breasts instead of two.

It's important to check if the bra is cutting into your back or is loose. Try on a new bra under a tight T-shirt to test this. Ideally you need to have a larger cup size and go bigger across the back. This will control and separate your breasts and give a good silhouette under clothes. Look for under-wiring for extra support and a rounded cup.

Big Thighs and Hips

A common problem with curvaceous hips is that knickers can dig in, giving a visible panty line. This can be ok with jeans but if you want to wear a sheer fabric, you need help.

A G-string may be comfortable but it will cut into your flesh and does nothing for your shape. Instead, go for knickers that sit comfortably around the hips without digging in.

Even better try support knickers that create a smooth silhouette from the waistline to halfway along the thighs. They redistribute the weight of the thigh and make them look slimmer and hold in the bottom, taking away the pear shape look.

How to do Lunch

Forget grabbing a quick sandwich, the art of lunching needs to be forever preserved. Even if you only do it once a year, knowing how to lunch is a pleasure that can be enjoyed at any age, by anyone.

You don't need to book the fanciest restaurant in town: putting a date in the diary and enjoying the ritual creates sense of occasion enough.

With your mum

Something of a time honoured tradition, lunch out with your mum usually takes place on a mother and daughter shopping day, when she comes to spend the day seeing your new flat or when you have something momentous to tell her.

But it's a great occasion for the women of the family to treat themselves and be waited on for a change.

Location: Choose somewhere up to date, but not scarily trendy, that will provide her with an experience that she can tell her friends about.

OR somewhere cosy with a traditional feel and great atmosphere, where you can take the time out to strengthen the mother-daughter bond.

Objective: Make her feel young again, up with the times, proud of you and profit from some one-to-one catch up time. Above all have fun!

NEVER TURN DOWN THE CHANCE FOR A GOOD
GIRLY GIGGLE OR A HEART TO HEART.

WITH WORK

So your boss asks you out to lunch. Most of us will immediately think 'Apart from work what will we talk about for an hour and a half?' or 'Why are they asking me out to lunch by myself – am I about to be sacked or is he going to make a pass at me?'

Location: Chances are your boss or an assistant will book the restaurant, but if you have a choice, go for somewhere relatively up-market that is formal without being stuffy and that isn't too intimate. Try to make sure it's somewhere that gets busy at lunchtime, that way if there are any awkward silences other people's chatter will cover them.

Objective: Instead of worrying about the event or thinking it's going to be the dullest occasion ever, try to make the most of some unexpected time with your boss. Always assuming you aren't going to be sacked, use it as an opportunity to tell them about the great things you've achieved and why you deserve a pay rise. It's also a great way to see a more human side to your boss and find out a bit more about what makes them tick. Improving your working relationship can only help your career.

WITH YOUR BEST MATE

Never turn down the chance for a good girly giggle or a heart to heart. Lunch with your best friend should always be a pleasure, never a chore.

Location: This can be anywhere you fancy. You can experiment with restaurants you've never been to, or have a picnic in the park. You know your friend and what she likes and if you make a mistake she'll forgive you.

Objective: Fun, fun, fun! And the chance to break the news and get her opinion on your latest major life decision – you're getting married, having a baby, have just broken up with your man or have bought some new shoes.

NETWORKING

The network lunch is the trickiest as you won't really know the person you're lunching with and must create an impression. But think of it in terms of an opportunity, a chance to meet someone new and enrich your life.

Location: This will depend on who's footing the bill. If it's you, go for somewhere comfortably within your budget that will still create an impression – an amazing pizza that tastes like it came straight from Naples will be as memorable as a three course extravaganza.

Make sure the atmosphere in the restaurant is right: it must have a buzz to cover potential silences and great service and sparkling tableware to give the impression of quality and care. Space around your table is also important – don't crowd your new contact.

Objective: To get your relationship off to a great start and to impress them by showing you've thought carefully about the venue and value the meeting. You will achieve your networking aims in a pleasant, enjoyable manner.

How to Get
a Great Haircut

**What's the first thing women do when
they break up with someone? Get a new
haircut. It's a classic 'hey I'm still
attractive, out with the old, in with the
new' tactic.**

....

This aside, if you're going to get an 'impact do',
how do you go about it without paying a fortune
to go to the latest coiffure to the stars?

How you choose to wear your hair says a lot about
you and your lifestyle. To help you avoid the tears
and tantrums that accompany hideous haircut hell
(and the added expense of buying a hat to cover it
up), here are a few common sense tips to help you
get a great haircut (you might want to pass them
on to your mum...):

◊ Find a good hairdresser. If you're stuck in a rut
with your hairdresser and don't think they can do
anything more exciting than a trim, CHANGE
THEM! You're not going to get a great 'do' from
someone who's as creative as a laboratory researcher

◊ Don't go for a whole new look with a brand new
hairdresser (well only if you're very brave). Instead
get them to do a couple of trims/tidy ups on your
hair first, before you take the plunge. This will
allow you to find out if they're any good and if you
trust them.

◊ Look at the salon they work in – is it efficiently run, clean and up to date? Ancient equipment, cracked sinks and soft-focus 1970s posters of hair models don't usually translate into a flair with the scissors

◊ Look at the hairdresser – do they cut with purpose, look you in the eyes, more importantly listen to what you want?

WHAT YOU CAN DO TO HELP
It's an old piece of advice but take a photo or picture from a magazine. It will give the hairdresser something to work from. But bear in mind, the haircut you leave with won't be an exact replica of the photo – be realistic. The texture of your hair and your face shape will make a difference to how the style ends up. Age and lifestyle are also factors.

Tell the hairdresser what you want and more importantly what you don't want. Don't be afraid to stop them half way through and get them to explain what they're doing. Use your hands to indicate where you'd like the hair to fall instead of just asking for an inch off the ends.

TIPS
◊ If you don't like the end result, tell them. It will usually be possible to do something about it

◊ Keep your options open, sometimes an unexpected urge to try something different can leave you with a haircut you might not have tried otherwise but that is perfect for you!

◊ Ask for styling advice – while the hairdresser styles your hair ask them for tips so that you can try and replicate the look at home

Impress instantly

It's something of a well-worn mantra that first impressions count. And it's true. But if you want to create an instant impression how do you go about it?

....

Your mother may have told you to be seen and not heard but that's not great advice if you want to create a fantastic initial impression.

Of course it depends who you are trying to impress but a few common sense rules apply:

Those vital first impressions
Research shows that 93% of our first impressions of a person are based on their appearance and body language, which makes dress, attitude and posture very important.

- Don't slouch, skulk, fidget or parade bad habits such as nail biting, sniffing or nose picking, all are a major turn off
- Dress appropriately for the occasion and if in doubt about matters of style, consult an expert
- Look people in the eye. Avoiding eye contact makes you appear shifty even if you're really only shy
- Walk tall and hold your head high – this creates an instant impression of confidence and general air of well being as well as improving posture
- Smile but don't grin like an idiot

Feeling comfortable in yourself
- Give yourself plenty of time to get somewhere

whether it be for an appointment at the dentist or a major job interview – arriving red faced, sweaty and flustered does not look good
- Wear comfortable underwear – fidgeting to get comfy or stopping to rearrange bra, knickers, tights is a big no-no
- Take care of yourself at all times. Exercise, regular maintenance of hair and nails will all contribute to a groomed, cared-for look and will show you're in control
- Practice social chitchat and interact with different types of people. A little bit of inane babble is a good way of buying time to get yourself together and will help establish a rapport

TIPS

◊ Project an 'accept me for who I am' message; people respect those who have the confidence to be themselves

◊ Don't try too hard. Going over the top screams lack of confidence and 'I need reassurance'

◊ Act interested and learn to be a good listener

◊ Be honest. Admitting you haven't heard of something or don't understand will win more points than if you pretend you know exactly what's what

◊ Don't talk too much. Gushing or giving your life story is not allowed

◊ Don't be a kiss arse. You don't need to agree with absolutely everything that's said. People will respect you for having your own opinion

Meet the Parents

Meeting your partner's parents is potentially fraught with problems.

....

Will you be good enough for his mum's precious darling? What if they don't approve of you? Or worse, what if you can't stand the sight of one another and wonder how these people could have produced the one you love? And what if you end up making a complete fool of yourself?

The reason why we get nervous is because we don't want to let our partner down. We want his parents' approval so that they give our relationship their blessing and are there to support us.

Still, there are a few ways to avoid the pitfalls:

◊ Be respectful of them and their lifestyle. No matter what sort of weird family habits you encounter, keep a straight face and avoid comment – after all, this family produced your beloved so they can't be that weird can they?

◊ Forewarned is forearmed – get the low down on his parents before you meet them and show a polite interest in golf or marmalade or whatever it is that they're passionate about. Also know which subjects to avoid – Auntie Susie running off with the woman next door isn't a good topic of conversation no matter how fascinating

◊ Actively seek ways to like and appreciate them – chances are you won't get them to change so learn to like them!

◊ Don't be too eager to please. Pretending you don't smoke when you're on 20 a day is a huge mistake – how will you explain your constant fidgeting and desire to walk the family dog every five minutes? Better to let them see the real you – well a watered-down, parents-in-law approved version anyway

◊ Don't tell in-law jokes. Even if you think they'll laugh it's not worth the risk and more often than not they're not funny anyway. You want them to think you have a good sense of humour don't you?

Shop Successfully

There are some skills that every woman should learn and shopping successfully is one of them. It's worth knowing how to get it right. Learn to spend your money well and experience that lovely post-shopping buzz.

◊ Make a list – this will help you focus on what you really want to buy rather than get distracted by other temptations and is especially important if you are on a budget. Don't write too many items on the list if shopping for clothes or for household items. Concentrate on getting the most important things first

◊ Remember the golden rules – the item must be the best quality you can find for your budget. It must represent value for money, be comfortable, fit well (if shopping for clothes) and be current but have more life in it than just one season

◊ Learn where to shop – ideally in the best places your budget will allow, which may mean going to new, different and out of the way places – worth it if you end up looking fab!

◊ Designer isn't necessarily best – not everything with a designer label is stylish or value for money. Learn to spot style and quality whether the item is designer or not

◊ Choose the right day – maybe this point's not so appropriate for a trip to the supermarket but for important clothes or furniture shopping you need to go on a day when you're not tired and have no time pressures

◊ Don't let pushy sales staff influence your decision-making process – ultimately only you know what's right for you

◊ Avoid temptations and old habits, stick to your list and if you do end up buying something you're unsure about (normally if in doubt don't buy it) ask what the returns policy is

◊ Sometimes realise you have to invest a little to get a lot back. As we spend about a third of our lives sleeping, buying a brilliant bed will never be a bad investment, the same goes for high-quality luggage, a designer court shoe or regularly shelling out on a fabulous haircut

Walk Like a Model

While most of us can never hope to be six feet tall, as thin as a rake and ultra-glamorous, learning to walk like a model is still within our grasp.

In the old days of debutantes, etiquette and deportment lessons, learning to walk like a model was considered essential. Naturally, walking model-like requires good posture – something many of us need to work on.

Posture

The secret of good posture is simple. Stand in front of a mirror and check out what's preventing you from standing up straight: are your shoulders hunched, your head poking forward like a tortoise, your back bent?

Then imagine a string is attached to the crown of your head and someone is pulling on it from above. Move your body accordingly and your spine will straighten, and your head will rise. Pull your shoulder blades together into the centre of your back and tuck your chin in slightly. Your should feel the back of your neck elongate, without losing any of the length in your spine. Now observe the difference!

Your ears, shoulders, hips, knees and ankles should form one straight line. Relax your shoulders and slightly bend your knees – you don't want to look like a robot. If you're standing for a long period of time, make sure to continue shifting your weight every so often.

PRACTICE WALKING IN HIGH HEELS BY LAYING A PIECE OF TAPE ON THE FLOOR IN A STRAIGHT LINE.

Your stomach and buttock muscles should tighten with correct posture and arms should be held loosely at your sides. This is the foundation on which you can build the habit of good deportment.

WALKING
With correct posture we can then learn to lift our

bodies up and forward with true muscle strength instead of being held up by our joints. This creates a much more fluid, graceful, and lofty movement pattern – the key to walking like a model.

Our weight is forward and balance becomes the method of lifting our bodies against gravity and we end up strengthening our bodies as a result.

Make sure your posture is still good – spine straight and tall, neck elongated, chin slightly downward and arms by your sides, buttock and stomach muscles taut. Correct posture while you're walking is the quickest way to look slimmer and taller – just like a model.

Then practice walking in high heels by laying a piece of tape on the floor in a straight line.

Starting with the right foot, place the heel on the line and the toe slightly off the line. When taking a step forward, move the back foot with the ankle passing the front leg's instep while the knee is bent.

When it becomes the front leg the knee straightens and the foot is gently placed on the straight line as before with the heel on the line. And don't forget to smile.

Once you've mastered this you're nearly there. Really you should also learn to pivot and turn as if you were on the catwalk – but who does that in real life?

RESULTS
A beautifully fluid, graceful walking style that will guarantee heads turning as you go by.

Whether to Let Him Pay

In these days of supposed equality some areas of etiquette have become confused. But good manners and a desire to impress should always be a given.

So when you're out for a first date with a man and the 'bill' question arises here's some advice.

If he's asked you out then there's an unwritten assumption that he'll pay. It's like you inviting people round to your house for dinner then expecting them to bring their own food. More than likely he'll have picked where you're going, making the onus on bill footing his. Relax, enjoy the meal then thank him prettily once it's finished.

Even today most men expect to pay on the first date – maybe it's the old 'provider' instinct kicking in or just a chance to show off.

If this makes you anxious though, a good way of making sure there aren't any awkward moments around bill paying is to let him take the lead with all the formalities – asking for menus, choosing the wine, etc. This will underline who's in the driving – and thus bill paying – seat.

If the thought of accepting a free meal from someone you barely know sends shivers down your spine, still try not to wade in with the 'I must pay my way, women earn as much as men, don't think

EVEN TODAY MOST MEN EXPECT TO PAY ON THE FIRST DATE.

you paying for the food entitles you to anything else' arguments.

Politely explain that as much as you appreciate the gesture, you'd feel much happier splitting the bill, or maybe suggest you take him out next time – only if you like him that is!

Bottom line, most women enjoy being taken out by a man. So why not just appreciate it for what it is – a compliment to you.

Write the Perfect Thank You Letter

In this age of mass information, email, text and phone the humble, hand-written thank you letter has unfortunately lost its popularity.

We can all remember our mum making us sit down after Christmas to write thank you letters to relatives with differing notions of seasonal generosity. But chances are we've forgotten how, or perhaps never knew in the first place.

Should we even bother writing a thank you letter? The answer is a resounding yes. As well as being good manners, the thank you letter is charming and remains one of the most gracious and often memorable ways of conveying appreciation.

Without getting all formal and foregoing the need for etiquette lessons, there are a few basics rules to remember when writing a thank you letter:

◊ Use high-quality writing paper, note cards or attractive postcards

◊ Address the person that you're thanking appropriately – it sounds obvious but a proper greeting sets the tone

◊ Express your gratitude in simple terms – the whole point of this letter is to create a simple expression of heartfelt sentiment. Don't worry about keeping it short and sweet, 'thank you for your hospitality' is a lot more effective and sincere than going into raptures about the décor in their guest bedroom

◊ Discuss what you're thanking them for – 'I put the flowers in the kitchen and they still look lovely after a week' is a nice way of showing that you didn't only appreciate the gift at the time. Even if you don't really like a gift or didn't enjoy an occasion there is generally something positive that you can say about it 'the venue for the party was lovely' or 'the woolly jumper you sent is a beautiful shade of pink'

◊ Mention the past and allude to the future – let the person you're thanking know how they fit into your life, for example, 'I'll call you soon but wanted to take time to say thanks' or 'I hear you're doing well in London, I hope we can get together soon'

◊ Sign off appropriately

Don't make this a letter about you and your news. It's about saying thank you and remember to keep it short and sincere

CHAPTER 2

Men

Find out if
He Loves You

These tips are by no means the definitive way of telling if he loves you but they might just help. And don't forget, with men actions often speak louder than words. You'll know he loves you if he:

....

◊ Lets you drive his new car

◊ Introduces you to all his friends and family and doesn't mind when they tell you tales of his misspent youth

◊ Assumes you're spending the weekend together

◊ Calls you often and for no particular reason

◊ Stops wearing his favourite T-shirt because he knows you hate it

◊ Wants to talk after sex

◊ Says he really likes you – probably means he thinks he's falling in love but doesn't want to say it because once it's out there, there's no going back

◊ Takes you to see the house he grew up in

◊ Calls you his girlfriend loudly, possessively and often to anyone who will listen

◊ In any given situation, considers your feelings before he acts

◊ Puts up with your quirks and obsessions even telling you he finds some of them 'adorable'

◊ Doesn't run a mile when you suggest Sunday lunch at your parents' house

FIVE SEX TIPS MEN LOVE AND HOW TO DO THEM

1. Nothing is more of a turn on to a man than knowing that you find him irresistibly sexy and want his body. So try not to come out with excuses when he's in the mood. Focus on getting yourself as into it as he is and you won't disappoint

2. Learn to be a really good kisser – of course practice makes perfect so pucker up at every opportunity. Think about what you're doing – don't just go for the full-on snog – tantalise with feathery kisses to his lips and face, make sure your lips are moist but not slobbery, soft but firm. Don't use your tongue like a sink plunger but lightly thrust it into his mouth, stroking his tongue and teeth, getting bolder to deepen the kiss. Use the kiss to indicate how you'd like sex to be, gentle and slow or fast and furious.

3. Give great oral sex – see p 58 Give the perfect blow job

4. Use the art of surprise – not strictly a 'how to' sex tip but a winner nonetheless. Not wearing underwear when he least expects it is always good or try getting a Brazilian or Hollywood and letting him discover it. When he least expects it, secretly let him know what you'd like to do to him in bed whether you're in the freezer aisle of the supermarket or at your parents' for dinner

5. Find the male G-spot. Rumour has it that focusing on the frenulum, the spot on the underside of the penis where the shaft is joined to the foreskin, is a big turn on. Happy hunting!

Giving Him the Elbow – Nicely

Breaking up with someone is never easy. In fact it could be said that it's nearly as bad as being dumped yourself. If you're thinking about saying goodbye to your man permanently (by dumping him that is not killing him), here are some ideas on how to give him the brush off without breaking his heart.

....

Giving the elbow after date one or two

You've only been out once or twice but you know you're not interested. But he is. He calls you wanting to go out again. If he leaves a message at home or on your mobile you may have escaped ever having to talk to him again. Because what you should do is ignore the call. Then as days stretch into weeks and you still don't ring back he can comfort himself with the reasons you may not have returned the call – you've moved abroad, had a fatal accident or moved house. Anything but the fact you've rejected him. He can brush it off lightly and move on.

If you do speak to him though, your best option – and I hate to say it – is to lie. Here's why:

Men have a persistence gene. If you simply say you're not interested chances are he'll take that as a challenge and pester you constantly trying to change your mind.

If, however, you lie and say that you've just got back with your old boyfriend then the door to everlasting happiness with you will slam in his face. He may see through this obvious excuse but will cling to it as a means of hanging on to his pride and telling himself that he really hasn't been dumped, it was just a case of circumstances that it didn't work out between you.

The distancing technique is another favourite. You explain how madly busy you are for the next few weeks, that your social life has gone crazy and that you'll call him when things calm down a bit. This isn't quite as good at the previous technique as it can throw out ambiguous signals but it's still effective and not too painful for the poor souls.

After a few dates

You quite liked him to start with but now you know that it's not going to happen. So how do you get rid of him? Again lying is a good option. In fact you can fall back on the old boyfriend excuse again. If you want to spare his feelings don't tell him you met someone else recently and it's going well. That will crush him and he'll feel like he's the loser in a competition. That's why the old boyfriend excuse is so great. You already knew him and just happened to find you were attracted to him again.

'There's just no chemistry between us' is another good standby. This is honest but not too hurtful. Most men won't be too affronted as it doesn't place the reason for your rejection totally on them.

AFTER YOU'VE BEEN GOING OUT FOR A WHILE

Sock it to him. It'll hurt but tell him the truth.
You've been going out for a while and he'll smell
an excuse a mile off. But you can be honest without
being cruel. Telling him he's rubbish in bed or
that he has personal hygiene issues is just being
downright mean.

Straight talking is what's needed here. Explain
your reasons carefully and let him have his say.
But stick to your guns so that he gets the message.

Don't try the 'we can just be friends' line. Everyone
knows that's crap. If you are going to be friends
with him in the future it will happen naturally
not just because you forced it out of the end of
your relationship.

So be gentle. And if you get really stuck, you can
always resort to lying.

Give the Perfect Blow Job

Now this is something your mother will never have taught you.

....

Five steps to male heaven

1. Once you've got him where you want him begin with some gentle teasing to let him know what your intentions are. Run your hands over the front of his trousers then bend down and gently bite him through the material. If his trousers have a zip you could pull it down with your teeth, very bold, but a great visual impact. Then pull his penis out of his trousers and tease him with your hands for a while before removing his trousers and underwear.

2. Before you get down to the serious stuff a bit more teasing never goes amiss. So use your mouth, hands and hair to create a true turn-on experience. Try letting your hair stroke against his penis and brush your lips up and down the shaft. Run the tip of your tongue up and down too – the general rule is to go up the shaft to the most sensitive part, the frenulum, and tease it with your tongue. This is the bit of skin that joins the foreskin to the head. Throughout this don't forget about his testicles. Use your hand to gently cup and squeeze them and follow by kissing and licking them.

3. You can only tease for so long and then it's time to get down to business. Take him into your mouth and let him feel the warmth and wetness of it, move his penis around, avoiding your teeth.

Position yourself so that it goes as deep as is comfortable by working with the angle of his penis and tilting your head accordingly. Then make a ring with your thumb and forefinger and put your hand to your mouth. This way your hand will supply the pressure and you won't get jaw ache. Then try one of these techniques:

- move up and down keeping your hand in the ring position on your mouth and the other cupping the testicles or gripping the base of his penis
- rotate the ring hand as you move your mouth up and down, swirling to increase the friction
- flick your tongue back and forth onto his penis, especially around the frenulum
- keep your other hand moving, caressing his testicles, belly and thighs

4. This stage is optional but for a little variety, and to prolong the sensations that your man will be experiencing, you could try removing your mouth from his penis and go back to teasing the head with your tongue. Blowing across the shaft will create a sexy shivery sensation with the cool air hitting the moist area your mouth has just left. But don't break contact with him, let your hands run up and down his chest and thighs.

5. By this stage he should be very close to orgasm and it's up to you what to do when he ejaculates. If you want him to climax in your mouth pulsate your hands in time with his ejaculation and then hold him in your mouth until he relaxes. You can keep a tissue handy if you don't want his sperm in your mouth afterwards. The other option is to get him to ejaculate on your breasts or bottom or even your face. When you feel his penis start to pulse, use your hands to direct it to the part of your body you think he'd like it to go.

Hold a
Bedroom Picnic

Forget what your mum told you about not eating in bed. It doesn't matter how many crumbs you get on the sheets, enjoy using your bedroom for a feast of delights.

....

GET PREPARED

Go to the supermarket on the look out for sexy aphrodisiac seduction foods. Try and incorporate some of the following:

- Aniseed, the Greeks and Romans thought the seeds increased desire, try a Kiss-me-quick cocktail with 45ml Pernod, two dashes aromatic bitters, four dashes Curaçao and soda water
- Asparagus, its phallic shape invites you to feed one another and it can be eaten suggestively
- Almonds are thought to arose passion in a woman; mix with honey, a touch of chilli powder and sea salt and roast in the oven for a fiery, sexy nibble
- Bananas are rich in potassium and B vitamins, which are necessary to produce sex hormones
- Chocolate, thought to affect neurotransmitters in the brain, is the ultimate sex food
- Raspberries and strawberries – perfect for feeding your lover they are often described in erotic literature as fruit nipples
- Oysters are the classic aphrodisiac – the Romans loved them and thought that they resembled the female genitals

SET THE SCENE

Go for a Lawrence of Arabia look with sumptuous fabrics, secret lounging areas and you as one of the harem feeding your sheikh.

- Swap your curtains for tumbling layers of sheer voile fabric in rich colours
- Cover the floor with all the cushions you can find, leaving a space for a tablecloth to spread out the food and cover the bed with a seductive satin bedspread
- Forget electric light and place tea lights all around the room to eat by candlelight
- Burn heady smelling incense to emphasise the exotic feel

ENTERTAIN

Invite your man into your lair and get him lounging on cushions.

- Pour him a drink and let him relax
- Position yourself in between him and the food and tempt him by feeding him treats from your aphrodisiac banquet
- When you are eating, lick and suck your food and fingers to show him your enjoyment of a sensual pleasure
- When you've finished eating, hint that the bed is a mere footstep away

How to Do
a Strip Tease

These instructions aren't going to turn you into an exotic dancer overnight but they will help you tantalise and impress your man.
....

What to wear
Beginning a striptease wearing provocative clothing has much more impact than starting off in your sexy lingerie straight away.

Separates such as a figure-hugging skirt and sexy top are best as they allow you not to give away all your secrets at once. It's even better if the top has buttons down the front – you can undo them one by one and leave the top hanging open for a while. Get him to help by allowing him to open one button at a time.

A pair of killer heels might not be easy to dance in but they'll look fantastic and a woman in sexy underwear and high heels is a guaranteed man pleaser. If you find it is too difficult to dance in them, you can kick them off once you've made your knockout entrance.

Music
You're looking hot. Now you need something to sway to and set the mood. Don't worry about the words of the song – let the beat do the talking. Pick music that sounds sexy to you.

By the end of the second song you should be down to your underwear. The third song and any others that come after it should be slow and stirring, the kind that make you feel like touching someone or being touched. It's best not to have any breaks between songs so do your preparation beforehand.

ACTION
Put a chair in the middle of the floor for your partner to sit in – a dining room chair works well, as he won't get too comfortable and will focus all

his attention on you. Place the chair facing away from the entrance to the room. Once he's sitting down, set the music going and make your entrance.

Eye contact is very powerful so get his attention and look him in the eyes as you come around to stand in front of him.

Dancing for someone does not mean bounding all over the room. Stand in front of him, close enough to touch fingertips with each other when your arms are extended, with your feet less than shoulder width apart.

Don't worry about fancy footwork and let your body interpret the music from your hips, outward.

As you start to strip remember to vary the speed at which you disrobe. Ease buttons out of their buttonholes and pull zips down slowly. Try to slide your clothes from your body.

Remember if you make yourself feel sexy, you'll look sexy. Think about how your clothes feel as you pull them across your skin. Look at your partner and think about the best sex that you've ever had.

Finally, while you're removing your underwear continue to tease by covering up what you're about to reveal next with your hands and arms.

THE GRAND FINALE
Reveal all slowly and move towards your partner. Tease away their wandering hands and straddle their lap.

What happens next is up to you!

How to Flirt
Successfully

Some people are naturally great flirts while others consider flirting to be either terrifying or the sign of being a slut.
···

Of course, it's neither. Those of you who flirt with men, women, the postman, your boss, anybody in fact – won't need this guide. But for the rest of us, who manage a tentative smile and eyelash flutter now and again, here's how. You'll be surprised how good flirting makes you feel.

Give clear signals
Let's face it men aren't great at interpreting signals from women. So if you start flirting make sure you know what you want, that your signals are clear and they convey what you mean. It's not fair to flirt with someone for the fun of it, unless they are obviously flirty themselves. If you genuinely want to meet people then by all means flirt but learn to separate sexual flirting signals from the 'hi I'm friendly' signals.

Feel good about yourself
Corny but true. Hoist your self-confidence up a notch and spread charisma. If you feel good about yourself, others will too.

Separate yourself from your friends
If you're out with a big girlie group or even just with a girlfriend, try to separate from them at some point so you appear more approachable. No

man wants to be rejected in front of a group of women and may hesitate to approach you when you are being 'protected' by them.

CHECK YOUR VOICE
Do you know what you sound like? Make sure that your voice is less nasal whine and more sensual waves of sound.

BE INTERESTING BY BEING INTERESTED
Don't talk too much about yourself but ask him open-ended questions. Most people love talking about themselves and are flattered when someone shows an interest.

GET NOTICED
If you worry about how to start conversations with strangers carry something to make it easier – that will make them notice you. Wearing unusual accessories or carrying an interesting book can often spark conversation.

MAKE THE FIRST MOVE
Lots of men say they would love to be approached by a woman. In these days of equality it's only fair we give it a shot!

BE YOURSELF
Don't assume a role because you'll be found out sooner or later. Be proud of who you are and if you're still uncertain work on it. There are loads of courses and self-help books out there.

GET OUT THERE
You can't be a great flirt if you're always at home in front of the telly. When you're invited out at work, go. If you've always wanted to learn to paint, do it and you could meet some like-minded people. If you're invited to a party where you know no one but the hostess, take a chance. You could meet someone great!

How to Invite
a Man Out

Men definitely like it when women ask them out. Why wouldn't they? But before you get asking, there are a few things you should know.

For starters, part of the guy will wonder if you've called him up because you want to have sex with him. Guys are generally hoping to have sex whenever they go on a date, so this probably won't mean he'll behave any different, but you might want to think about setting some limits early on – unless that is why you called him.

Also, be prepared for lots of dating grey areas: Who'll drive? Who'll pay? Who'll decide where to go? Normally the impetus falls with the man to control the flow of events on a date, but if you've asked him out how far will your initiative extend? You need to decide how much of the date to dictate.

Finally – something that men have got used to over the years – you could ask someone out only for the answer to be no. So be prepared for it.

Hot tips to ask him out

◊ Don't wait for men to approach you. Be a flirt! Make the first move. Guys will be so relieved and flattered that they'll usually flirt back, buy you a drink or ask you out

◊ Choose a pulling outfit that shows that you're available but don't try too hard or you'll look

desperate. Go for either cleavage or legs and leave
the rest to the imagination. While he's mesmerised
by your assets take a chance and ask him out

◊ Hit the bar – it's a great place to chat up men
while you wait to get served. Initiate conversation
here and you've established a contact that you can
play on later in the evening. If you plan it so you
talk to him again he'll know you're interested. If
he's responsive it's the perfect opportunity to ask
him out

◊ Be bold – if you're in a restaurant and have been
making eye contact with a man, send him a note
via the waiter, to be delivered after you leave,
asking if he wants to go for a drink sometime and
leaving your phone number

◊ Watch his body language – a great way to check
if he likes you before you take the plunge and ask
him out. Any of the following will let you know if
he's interested:

– his legs are crossed and the top leg points
  towards you

– he squares his body when you look over –
  chest out and straightens up

– his lips part when you first lock eyes

– he tries to attract your attention, whether by
  subtly adjusting his tie or doing a handstand

READ HIS MOODS

Let's face it, men aren't the natural communicators that women are. Often they find it hard to say what they mean.

Sometimes he may simply just not want to talk about anything. But often although he seems distant he's secretly longing to tell you how he feels but doesn't know how. So try to learn to read his moods.

THE SILENT TREATMENT
Often this simply means he's thinking hard about something. As we girls know, men aren't great at doing more than one thing at once. So if he doesn't respond, can't chat or answer your questions about what you should wear to your best friend's party, it's because he's deep in thought and wants to finish his thinking before he moves on to something else.

Solution: Don't point out that he hasn't said a word for hours as this could make him withdraw even more but say that you're there if he wants to talk about anything. Hopefully knowing that he can chat when he's ready will make him more likely to do so.

IT'S IN HIS LOOK

If he glances away as soon as you catch his eye, it probably means he needs your emotional support but is trying to pick the perfect moment to tell you what's on his mind.

Solution: Arrange a quiet night in for the two of you. Don't watch TV and ignore the phone. Plan an intimate dinner so that you can look him in the eyes across the table and take time to re-establish the connection between you. By creating the perfect setting for confidential discussion, he'll feel much more able to talk about the issue that's been troubling him.

BODY LANGUAGE

If you notice he's folding his arms or covering his face with his hands, your man is trying to cover up the fact that there's anything wrong. He's using classic body language to protect himself.

Solution: Sit down beside him while he's relaxing, take his hands in yours and gently ask him what's wrong. Without his hands to hide behind his defences will be down and he should find it easier to tell you what's up.

Seduce Your Man

To seduce is to tempt or entice into sexual activity. It's a kind of dance, where moves are made by each person to coax the other into bed. And there are many ways it can be done. Here are a few ideas.

....

TRADITIONAL

Champagne, flowers and romance are the three accompaniments to the traditional seduction. This approach is classic but predictable. However it can be elevated to something special by the care with which you go about it. When your man gets home, a trail of rose petals leading from the front door to the living room where you've laid out a beautiful feast in front of the fire will wow his senses. Feed each other – no knives and forks allowed – and constantly kiss and touch. As the temperature rises lead him into a candlelit bedroom and slowly undress him. Pour some champagne onto his body, lick it off and look forward to what follows.

GO SLOW

At a party or dinner tantalise him with sexual gestures but don't let him touch you. Lean over him and show him your cleavage or look him in the eyes, reach around and hold your hair away from the back of your neck pushing your breasts forward. Smooth your outfit suggestively down your body. After a few hours of look but don't touch he'll be desperate to get his hands on you. Hold him off for as long as possible to ensure an explosive reaction when he gets you home.

LITTLE WIFE

You may have no intentions of getting married or may be married already but don't underestimate the sexiness of domesticity. It's the classic one-two – show a man how well you can take care of him and fulfil his sexual needs. Make the house sparkle and cook a delicious meal. Sit him down and perform the smallest tasks for him such as grating parmesan on his pasta and spreading a napkin on his lap. Wear wholesome but subtly suggestive clothes – snug sweatpants with a get-me-on-the-sofa midriff baring top. Lean over him while you serve him and let your body brush his. And then on to dessert...

SHOCK TACTICS

Always a good one to liven things up. Leave him a downright dirty answer message and tell him you've got a hotel room booked and are waiting for him in the reception of his office now. Or, get him into your car and blindfold him. Drive to a secluded outdoor location and then seduce him. Take off the blindfold halfway through the experience. The shock of discovering where he is and you having your wicked way with him will blow his mind.

SENSE – ATIONAL

Use the five senses as your inspiration for a seduction experience. Start with music, scented candles, a dimly lit bedroom and a turn-him-on-outfit. Move it up a gear by blindfolding him and feeding him tempting treats. Touch his body and make him guess what you are using – a feather, a soft brush (a make-up brush) or the ends of your hair. Murmur sexily what you'd like to do to him and have him do to you. Let nature take its course.

Take the Initiative in Bed

You might be full of initiative already but for those who need a little help a few sex assertiveness tips follow:

1. Turn up the heat – setting the scene and easing yourself into taking the leading role will help you be more confident later on. Send him sexy text messages throughout the day; lift up your skirt so that he can see the new hold ups you've bought; cook dinner for him wearing just an apron.

2. Let him know you want it – don't be coy, send out specific signals that you want to get him into bed, lick your lips, hold eye contact, touch his hand, arm and thigh, whisper what you'd like to do to him.

3. Get him naked first – staying fully clothed while he's displayed as nature intended will give you an enormous sense of confidence and inspire you to have your wicked way with him on your terms.

4. Play the dominatrix – getting into the role of a woman who makes men do her bidding sexually will mean you have him exactly where you want him. The fact that you're role playing should mean that you can order him to satisfy you in ways you wouldn't have dared to before.

5. Surprise him – one way of taking the initiative is to try something you've never done before such as a new position or dressing up.

6. Jump his bones – if he doesn't get the subtle approach just try the full on one, greet him naked as he comes home from work and don't take no for an answer or go up to him at a party, grab him and give him a passionate kiss – he'll soon get the message.

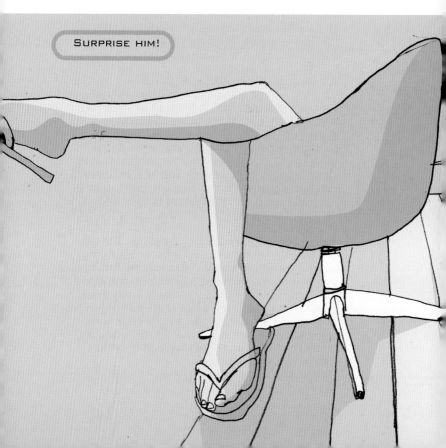

What to Wear in Bed

Famously when asked what she wore in bed, Marilyn Monroe replied, 'Chanel No. 5'. Of course what you wear will depend on your personality and taste in general, not to mention whether you are sleeping alone or not.

To anyone who is sleeping in an ancient T-shirt and a pair of men's boxer shorts take note – it's time to change your ways. What kind of impression are you trying to give out?

Banish grotty grey PJs and take note.

Seduction scene
Always keep something on hand to slip into should the need to seduce arise. Luxury fabrics like silk, satin and lace are key when picking out this type of nightwear. Short or long it should cling lovingly to your body and be a pleasure to touch. Baby doll sets are also good – keep them feminine and sexy rather than tarty and obvious.

Comfort zone
You can be comfortable and feminine. The key is not to buy old woman pyjamas or anything bearing motifs of kittens or angels that will make you look about twelve and at a sleepover. Avoid floor-length tent nighties – deeply unsexy and reminiscent of Great Auntie Hilda and anything in synthetic fabrics. You'll crackle ominously every time you move. Instead go for lounging pants style with snug vest top or T-shirt or cute little shorts in the summer.

GO YOUR OWN WAY

Some people sleep naked. Fine but chilly if your house burns down and you have to wait outside with the firemen. But then this might be your idea of heaven.

CHAPTER 3

BAKING, HOMEMAKING AND BEING A domestic goddess

Achieve Work-Life Balance

True work-life balance is hard to achieve but the following advice should help ensure a healthier and happier lifestyle.

....

Know your time demands

A good way to find out how much time each activity in your life takes up and how that affects you is to take a piece of paper and write your name in the middle. Then think of a typical day and tear off a bit of paper for every activity you do. The more stressful the demand on you, the larger the piece of paper you should tear. This will help show you what things cause you stress and how much time you are leaving for yourself.

Find some me-time

By looking at the bits of paper you've just torn up you should have a good idea of how you spend most of your time. Work – be it in an office or as a full time mother – will probably take up the largest part. Now take another piece of paper but this time start by thinking about how much paper you'd like to be left with when you've finished tearing – i.e. how much me-time you'd like. Then make it a priority to re-juggle and delegate other activities and responsibilities to ensure you work towards your ideal me-time goal.

Live in the present

It's easy when you're stressed out to think about everything you have to do and worry about when you're going to have time to do it. But if you're always thinking about what's coming next you won't live for the moment. Next time you find your mind racing stop and think, 'Where am I?' This should help you focus on what's happening now. Thinking about the past and what could happen in the future is futile, as the only place you can enjoy and take action is the present.

TIPS

◊ Set the same exit time from work every day and only stay late during real crisis periods. If you don't leave on time you won't have any time left for me-time and your stress levels will rise

◊ Try and plan a social activity at least once a week and make it a rule not to cancel. Forcing yourself to do something different helps you recharge mentally

◊ Don't discuss your work at home or complain for hours about all the things that you have to do. This just makes your mind more restless when you should be relaxing. If you need to vent your feelings, limit any discussion to five minutes only

◊ Don't forget to dedicate some time to your relationships – to do this properly you must try and put your work and other responsibilities to one side

Bake a Cake

In our mother's era baking a cake was considered a basic skill. Nowadays we tend to buy rather than make things like cakes, pastry and puddings. But cake making is very easy and will impress anyone you invite round for afternoon tea.

Sponge cake

Pre-heat the oven to 180°C/Gas mark 4. Butter a sandwich tin 21cm in diameter and just under 5cm deep.

For a small sponge you will need:

- 125g sugar
- 125g self-raising flour
- 125g butter
- 2 eggs

If you want to make a bigger sponge or two halves to sandwich together with jam and whipped cream then use 225g each of sugar, flour and butter with 4 eggs.

You can also add flavourings to this basic sponge – 1 teaspoon vanilla extract or the zest of a lemon or orange.

If you have a food processor this cake is really easy. Simply put all the ingredients into the processor and mix until smooth. Alternatively, put all the ingredients into a bowl – making sure the butter is soft – and beat by hand using a wooden spoon until the mixture is smooth. Sifting the flour will give the cake an extra lightness but is not strictly necessary.

Then spread the mixture into the pre-buttered sandwich tin and bake for 25 minutes. When the cake is ready the top should spring back when pressed and a skewer inserted into the cake should come out clean.

Sprinkle with a dusting of caster sugar and serve with a nice cup of tea.

Be the Perfect Hostess

What woman doesn't dream of being the perfect hostess? If all your mother could do was wheel out a few cocktail sausages and change the hand towels in the bathroom here are the ten commandments of perfect hostessing:

....

1. Being gracious and charming may not come naturally but both are attributes you need to cultivate as the perfect hostess. It's not about impressing people but making them happy to be in your company and your home.

2. Always remember that guests will only be as relaxed as their hostess so having a little Dutch courage before they arrive is no bad thing. And don't be too polite, no one is going to have fun if they constantly think they have to mind their manners.

3. Make sure everyone feels included. Mix in old social retainers with new guests to ensure sparkling conversation.

4. Always have on hand a good supply of long shelf-life, easy-to-prepare snacks and a range of drinks – soft and alcoholic – for those who may drop in unexpectedly. The basics to whip up into an informal dinner or the number of a great local takeaway that you

can then displace into gorgeous dishes will make you a hostess who is never fazed.

5. Don't use the same formula twice for the same guests and try to introduce an element of surprise into your gatherings, however small, such as an ice sculpture or an 'invent your own cocktail' game.

6. For a major event a good hostess will plan like a general – creating the guest list, menu, drinks, supervising glassware and decoration and when in doubt will hire professionals to help out.

7. Aside from getting the guest mix right, a good maxim for a dinner party is: cold room, hot plates and low table decorations.

8. Imitation is a great way to success – if you go to a great dinner party or event ask yourself why and try to replicate that at home.

9. Don't be afraid of letting your personality shine through – a great hostess may express all the individuality she wants while a good guest should try to leave as good an impression on the hostess as possible so that they're invited back again on another occasion.

10. Try your best to be witty and amused and make sure that Mr or Mrs Sad Person married to your best friend feels that the party has been made for them – after all being a hostess isn't terminal, you can go back to your real life the next day.

Change a Nappy

The basics
◊ Wash and dry your hands

◊ Set up a warm, clean, dry, area to change the baby. You can use a changing mat, but a towel or clean cloth nappy on any soft, warm surface is fine

◊ Prepare your supplies. If using disposable nappies, you'll need a clean nappy and a plastic bag; if you've opted for terry nappies, you'll need a clean one, safety pins and plastic pants

◊ If the baby has, or is prone to, nappy rash, you'll also want to have some barrier cream or petroleum jelly to hand.

Changing a disposable nappy
◊ Take the clean nappy and unfasten the nappy tabs, fastening them back on themselves so they don't stick to your baby. Don't remove the dirty nappy yet

◊ Unfasten the dirty nappy and wipe away any excrement with the nappy, taking care to cover the penis with a clean cloth or nappy if your baby is a boy – for sanitary reasons and to avoid a warm shower!

◊ Grasp the baby's ankles in one hand and lift its bottom off the table

◊ Fold the dirty nappy in half under the baby, unsoiled side up and remove it

◊ Use a baby wipe or wet cloth to clean the baby's

front thoroughly. For a girl, always wipe from front to back — away from her vagina. This will help to reduce the possibility that bacteria will get into her vagina and cause an infection

◊ Continuing to lift the baby's legs, clean his/her bottom well

◊ Swap the clean nappy for the dirty one. The clean nappy's top half (the half with the tabs) should go under the baby's rear, and the bottom half should come up between his/her legs, which should be spread as widely as is comfortable. Try not to bunch the nappy between the baby's legs – it can cause chafing and discomfort. For boys, tuck the penis down so moisture will be less likely to escape

◊ Fasten the nappy at both sides with the tapes, making sure it's snug, but not so tight that it pinches his/her skin. Check the manufacturer's instructions for specific tips

◊ Using the tapes on the nappy, re-tape the soiled nappy around the contents, put it in a plastic bag and in the bin

◊ Dress your baby and finish off by washing your hands thoroughly

CHANGING A TERRY CLOTH NAPPY

First fold the nappy:

◊ Spread out the nappy. Fold one third of the width from the left edge towards the centre

◊ Now do the same from the right edge leaving a strip one third of the width of the original cloth. The nappy should now be three layers thick

◊ Fold one third up from the bottom so you have a six-ply thickness. Position this area in the front for a boy; for a girl, place it under her rear

To change the nappy:
◊ Unpin the old nappy, wipe any excrement away with the dirty nappy and put it aside. Use a baby wipe or wet cloth to clean the baby's bottom thoroughly

◊ As with the disposable nappy, grasp the baby by the ankles and lift up his/her bottom. Place a clean nappy under the baby. Make side flaps by flaring out the fabric you folded at the top of the back half of the nappy

◊ Pull the side flaps forwards from the back of the nappy and bring them together at the front so that they meet on the baby's stomach

◊ Place two fingers under the nappy fabric to avoid pricking the baby and insert a nappy pin away from the baby's navel, through the layers of towelling and out the other side. Fasten the pin

◊ Tip any waste from the soiled nappy into the toilet. Put the used nappy in a nappy bucket and close the lid tightly. Wash the nappies in a separate load. Use hot water, double rinse and avoid fabric softeners or anti-static products, as they can irritate a baby's sensitive skin

◊ Dress your baby and finish off by washing your hands thoroughly

How to Iron a Shirt

The days of being the 'little woman' are long gone and men are supposed to know how to iron their own shirts. But still, it's useful to know how a shirt should be ironed – either to make your own wardrobe look beautifully pressed or to treat your beloved (on the odd occasion) to the feeling of a crisp, crease-free shirt on his back.

So if your mother never showed you how, here's a step by step guide:

Make sure your ironing board is at a comfortable height for you to work at – about hip level should ensure that your arm is slightly bent when ironing and not carrying the whole weight of the iron.

If you're ironing a pure cotton shirt, the iron should be on its hottest temperature setting. Most irons mark this setting for cotton and linen.

Other shirt fabrics, such as polyester-cotton mixes, require a medium hot iron while synthetics need a cool iron.

A damp cotton shirt is easier to iron than a bone dry one so spraying or sprinkling the shirt with water before you begin is recommended.

If your iron has a steam setting, fill up the water reservoir in the iron and switch on the steam.

Arrange the shirt on the ironing board with the buttons facing you and the sleeves spread out to your right and left. Smooth out the inside of the collar and move it to the centre of the ironing board, as this is what you will be ironing first.

When the iron has heated up – you must wait for it to do this, you won't eliminate creases successfully with a semi-warm iron – start by ironing the inside of the collar to where it joins the rest of the shirt.

Next turn the shirt over and look for the section of fabric that sits across the shoulders on a man's shirt (you can also iron women's shirts like this but you generally won't have a separate section of fabric). Called the yoke, it's cut separately and runs across the top of the back of the shirt. Just beneath it, leading from the middle is usually a pleat that runs into the length of the back of the shirt.

Spread out this top shoulder section and iron it, pushing the tip of the iron into the corners where the sleeves are joined and taking care not to let the bottom of the iron crease the section underneath where the pleat begins.

Once this is done turn the shirt around again in order to iron the front half of the shirt, starting with the side with the buttons on it.

Place the shirt over the rounded tip of the ironing board so that the collar hugs the tip and you can

smooth down the front half with the buttons over
the board. Iron this half.

Re-position the shirt in the same way so that you
can iron the other half of the shirtfront.

Now turn the shirt over and iron the bottom half of
the back of the shirt, again hooking the collar over
the rounded end of the ironing board to hold it in
place and smoothing out the back of the shirt.

Finally iron the sleeves. Iron the inside of the cuffs
first and then smooth out the first sleeve in the
middle of the ironing board. Iron towards the cuff,
pulling on the cuff while you iron to straighten out
the sleeve if necessary. Turn the sleeve over and iron
the other side. Do the same for the other sleeve.

Slip your crease-free shirt on to a hanger and fasten
the top button. The shirt is now ready to wear.

Make Marmalade

To make about 10lb (4.5kg) of Seville Orange
Marmalade:

  3lb Seville Oranges
  2 lemons
  5–6 pints water
  6lb preserving or granulated sugar
  knob of butter

Seville oranges are available from the end of
January for two to three weeks. They are
considered to be the best oranges for marmalade
because of the deep-coloured skins and good
proportion of pips, which provide plenty of pectin
for a good set.

If you can't get Seville oranges you can use any
bitter orange or combination of grapefruit, lemons
and oranges.

You will need to have a heavy-based saucepan or
preserving pan made of aluminium or stainless
steel and a square of muslin in which you will
collect the pips.

Method

Scrub and dry the oranges and lemons. Cut them
in half and squeeze out all the juice. Have a small
plate at hand with a square of muslin on it so that
as pips collect in the squeezer you can place them
on the muslin.

With a teaspoon, scoop out the loose membrane
from the centre of each squeezed orange and place
it with the pips on the muslin.

Then use a sharp knife to shred the skins as coarsely or finely as you like. These will provide the 'shred' in your marmalade.

Place the shredded rind in a large bowl with the juice and the pips and pith tied in the muslin and half the water. The quantity of water will depend on whether you have a narrow deep pan, in which case use five pints of water as there will not be so much evaporation, or a wide shallow pan – six pints are recommended for this.

Allow these ingredients to soak for several hours or overnight if possible. After soaking transfer them to the pan, add the remaining water, then bring to the boil and allow to simmer steadily for 1.5–2 hours or until the peel is quite tender and the quantity is reduced by half. Use the handle of a wooden spoon to measure this rather than guess. Squeeze the muslin bag against the side of the pan to extract the pectin.

Add the sugar and stir over a gentle heat till dissolved. When the sugar has been added the pan should not be more than half full to allow for a good rolling boil and to avoid boiling over.

Then, and only then, bring the marmalade to the boil and cook over a high heat for about 15–20 minutes until setting point is reached (see below).

Stir in the knob of butter to disperse the scum and allow to cool for 15 minutes before pouring into warm, dry jars. Cover and seal either when very hot or when quite cold. Label and store in a cool dry place.

◊ Don't add the sugar before the skin of the fruit is tender. It can harden the skin if added too early. Always stir over a gentle heat until the sugar has completely dissolved before allowing the marmalade to come to the boil

◊ If you have a cooking thermometer it will include the setting point for jam and marmalade. Alternatively the cold plate test is simple and reliable. Always take the pan off the heat while making this test

◊ Place a teaspoonful of marmalade on a clean, cold saucer and leave in a cold place for one minute. If it is ready the surface of the marmalade will look as though it has a skin on it. Push the blob using the side of your finger. If the skin forms permanent wrinkles the setting point has been reached

Make the Bed

In these days of duvets and comforters, using sheets and blankets may seem a touch old-fashioned. But on the odd occasion when you might have a guest and no duvet and have also run out of fitted sheets, knowing how to make a bed properly is invaluable.

◊ Spread a flat sheet over the mattress, making sure the edges hanging over the bed are not longer on one side than the other or at top or bottom

◊ Tuck the end of the sheet under the head of the bed first then go to the end of the bed and tuck that in, leaving the side flaps of the sheet hanging down. Ensure both ends are tucked in tightly and pulled taut along the length of the bed

◊ Go back and stand on one side at the head of the bed. To tuck in the first side of the sheet, use the hospital corner method. This is a good method to ensure the sheet does not come untucked easily and stays taut across the bed. Pull up the side of the sheet near the top of the bed where it falls at the corner so that it rests on the mattress in the shape of a triangle

◊ Tuck in the flap still hanging down over the edge of the bed then fold back the triangular portion of sheet resting on the mattress so that it hangs over

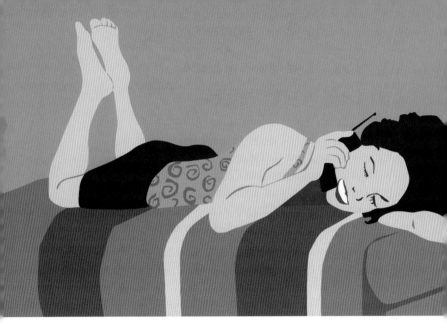

the edge of the bed. Tuck this in and you should have the perfect hospital corner

◊ Repeat this all around the bed and repeat the whole process again with the top sheet and blankets using hospital corners for all of them. The hemmed end of the top sheet should be at the headboard end of the bed, and the hem should be about a foot from the headboard when the sheet is folded back

◊ Position the pillows at the head of the bed before tucking in the top sheet. The top of the blanket should lay a couple of inches below the top of the sheet

◊ Then simply fold down the sheet and blanket and leave the pillows exposed

◊ Finish off the bed with an attractive bedcover

Make Your Bedroom a Boudoir

The dictionary definition of boudoir is a woman's small private room or bedroom. These days many of us are lucky to have a spare room for guests let alone an extra room that we can transform into our own private space.

....

But with a little imagination you can make your bedroom into a boudoir that is both decadent and inviting. It should be the perfect place to grab some me-time or set the scene for seduction.

Decide on your scheme

Whether you're going to totally redecorate or merely add a few feminine touches it's important to decide on the look you are going for. Look around you at the way your home is currently decorated and at how you dress. Do you go for the traditional look or contemporary? Do you like floral prints or an eclectic mix of styles? Is sixties retro your thing or are you in love with Art Deco? Do you prefer formal or informal?

Trying to pinpoint your style will help you decide on a look for your boudoir. It will also help set the mood. If in doubt ask your friends or family how they see you as this will help you focus on your personal style.

De-clutter

You cannot feel sensual, calm and at home in your own space if clutter surrounds you. Sort through the mess and throw some of it away. If that's not possible, invest in a new hide-all wardrobe (to complement your scheme of course) or some attractive storage boxes or closed cupboard with shelving. If you have a TV in your bedroom, banish it. Lying watching TV will do nothing to promote the exploration of the senses that being in your boudoir will encourage.

Colour
To some extent your choice of style may dictate the colours you go for in your boudoir. But it's important to remember that this is a sensory experience, designed to make you and whoever you're entertaining relax. So no harsh, jarring colours allowed. Whether you go for a bold, pastel or neutral palette the colours should be warm and soft in tone.

Texture
This is what will bring together the sensory aspects of the room and enhance the colours and style you have chosen. Pick accessories for the room that are gorgeous to touch – even if you are not redecorating, a beautiful rug, velvet curtains or a cashmere cushion can introduce sensuality into a room. Let your imagination run riot – silk, wool, smooth natural wood, organza or gauzy voile beg to be touched.

Lighting
Lighting should be soft and flattering – think candlelight and side lamps with pretty shades or a softly glowing chandelier.

Finishing touches
Once your boudoir is decorated you'll need to set the scene. Again think of the five senses. Scented candles, evocative music and some exotic foods will complement and enhance the atmosphere you have created. Just add the man of your choice.

Pack for
a Long Weekend

**We girls aren't exactly known for
travelling light so learning how to pack
for the weekend is an invaluable skill.
Follow and adapt these top tips:**

◊ Leave your supersize suitcase in the attic. It is
possible to pack everything you need for a weekend
getaway in one overnight bag

◊ Pack shoes and boots first – two pairs should
suffice, one that is good for walking in and a
dressier pair for evenings out. If you're going to the
country a further pair of old trainers or walking
boots may be necessary for outdoor activities

◊ Use the shoes to help co-ordinate your clothing
colour scheme. Black and denim are useful for
trousers and skirts as they go with anything. Navy
and neutrals like beige are also good. Choose
fabrics that don't wrinkle but hold their shape well,
such as raw silk, knit jersey or cotton with Lycra™

◊ Make the most of the space you have by shoving
anything you don't mind wrinkling – socks,
underwear, nightie – into your shoes. Fold other
clothes as flat as possible

◊ Think layering – a white cotton vest with a shirt
on top can then be topped with a jumper, cardigan
or jacket for extra warmth or worn on its own
should the weather be hotter

◊ Great accessories are the way to make your outfits exciting – statement jewellery, belts, scarves and a classic handbag and evening clutch purse do not take up much room and can change and update an outfit instantly

◊ Leave behind the bathrobe, hairdryer and umbrella – you can always borrow these things from your hotel or your hostess

◊ A multipurpose jacket or coat is ideal as it can be worn for both day and evening – smart-casual leather jackets are great. If you're really stuck, and weather permitting, pack a pashmina or shawl-like cover up to go with your evening wear as it won't take up much room

ALL YOU NEED FOR A CITY WEEKEND
Jeans / casual trousers or skirt for the day; a dressier skirt or smart black trousers for evening; a thin sweater or microfleece cardigan in a bright colour and four tops including a shirt and a dressy evening top.

For a country or beach escape, fine-tune your city outfit as follows:

Add a pair of shorts, a sun hat, a bikini/bathing suit and a sundress that can also be used as a beach cover-up.

IT IS POSSIBLE TO PACK EVERYTHING YOU NEED FOR A WEEKEND GETAWAY IN ONE OVERNIGHT BAG.

Plant a Window Box

For those living in flats with no garden space or even a terrace or balcony, a window box is an excellent way to grow things. Even for those with a garden, window boxes can enhance the outside of the house and are easy to change for a seasonal look.

Choose your window and box

If your windows open outwards you will not be able to have a window box on the sill. Metal brackets fitted below the window will support the box so that any growth will come to sill level.

Brackets should be screwed into wall plugs in walls made of brick or mortar and must be sturdy enough to carry the heavy weight of container, moist compost and plants. If in doubt, get a professional to fit them for you.

You must also think about access for watering, easy if the windows are on the ground floor and you can water from outside but make sure window boxes are easily accessible for watering from upstairs windows.

You can choose a box made from terracotta, wood, plastic or concrete depending on the look you are going for and the sturdiness of your window sill.

A window box, furnished with several draining holes, is generally about 15–20cm deep and wide and, unless purpose built, in lengths up to about

120cm. So don't forget to measure your window sill before you buy a box!

Ensure they are raised slightly on small blocks so that water can drain away easily – on upper windows you might want to put the blocks in a drip tray with the window box on top to avoid water dripping on passers by.

PLANT THE WINDOW BOX
Depending on the time of year the plants in your window box will vary but the basics are the same.

◊ Get together everything you'll need – plants, a trowel, bag of soil-less compost, some handfuls of crocks or expanded clay granules for drainage, a rigid plastic liner with drainage holes to fit the window box if you are using one. A liner is type of plant container that sits inside the window box itself. You don't need to use one and can plant directly into the window box but the advantage is that you can simply remove the liner once the flower display is ended and put another in its place already planted up

◊ Put large or heavy window boxes in place before you plant them

◊ In the bottom of the window box or liner, if you are using one, put a layer of crocks or other coarse material such as the clay granules to prevent drainage holes becoming blocked

◊ Partly fill the liner or box with compost

◊ Knock plants out of their pots and as they are planted in the window box or liner work compost around them eventually topping up compost to just

below the rim of the box. Don't water the box until
it is in its permanent position

◊ Raise boxes that do not have liners on to blocks
about 2cm high to allow free drainage

◊ Water and enjoy the fruits of your labour

Tips
◊ Plants for summer: verbena, border carnations,
lobelia, osteospermums, petunias, pelargoniums,
dwarf tobacco plants, fuchsias, geraniums and
Helichrysum petiolare, *Impatiens* (busy lizzie)
and herbs

◊ Plants for spring – shorter-growing bulbs do
well, such as dwarf daffodils, Dutch crocuses
and hyacinths, which you could combine with
trailing ivy

◊ For year-round planting – try evergreen dwarf
shrubs and ivy

Set a dinner table

For those occasions when you want to impress it's important to know how to lay a proper formal dinner table.

··

The basic settings

◊ Allow 24–30in for each place setting to avoid over-crowding

◊ Place settings should be 1in from the edge of the table

◊ The bread plate should be placed to the left of the place setting

◊ All cutlery is placed around the place setting in the order of use. What is to be used first is placed farthest from the plate

◊ Knives are placed to the right of the plate, with the knife's cutting edge facing the plate. However, a small knife for butter spreading should be placed diagonally on the bread plate, with the blade edge toward the dinner fork

◊ All forks are placed to the left of the plate, in order of use

◊ A cup and saucer are not part of a formal place setting. They should be brought to the table along with the teaspoon and the dessert plate

◊ Don't forget about the napkin. Arrange a folded napkin down the centre of the top plate. If a soup bowl is set on the top plate, then place the folded napkin to the left of the forks

Setting the table

Firstly prepare the table. Make sure you have the right number of chairs for your guests. Align them so they are spaced evenly down one side of the table placing a corresponding chair on the other side of the table so that your guests will be facing one another, using the head and end of the table if necessary.

If you use a tablecloth, make sure it is evenly spread over the table and immaculately pressed. Or place table mats directly on to the surface of the table. If you have large mats, cutlery will sit on the outside edges of the mat. If the mats are small, cutlery sits on either side.

At formal dinner parties a service plate or charger is set at each guest's place then taken from the table when the first-course plates are removed. When served, dinner plates are then placed on top of the charger. If you're not using a service plate, then set dinner plates at each setting.

Serving salad

If salad is served as a first course, place the salad plate on the dinner plate. If table space allows, the salad plate can be arranged to the left of the forks.

If salad is to be served European style, after the entrée, place the salad fork to the right of the place fork, next to the plate. If you are setting a salad knife, place it on the right of the plate to correspond with the placement of the salad fork.

Serving soup

If you are serving soup, the soup bowl sits on top of the service plate as ideally soup is served at the table.

Place knives are set to the immediate right of the dinner plate, blades facing the plate. The soup spoon goes to the right of all knives. Forks are placed to the left of the dinner plate in the order of their use, from the outside toward the plate.

SERVING DESSERT
Dessert spoons and forks can be placed horizontally above the dinner plate or can be brought to the table with the dessert plates.

SETTING GLASSES

Water goblets should be set just above the top of the place knife. The wine glass, red or white, is placed slightly to the right of the water goblet. When using both red and white wine glasses, place them to the right of the water goblet, red then white.

Place a champagne flute behind the other two wine glasses, forming a triangle.

BE THE LIFE
AND SOUL OF A PARTY

How do they do it, those girls who are constantly surrounded at parties, the centre of a group having the best time in the world?

◊ **Be yourself** – someone who genuinely likes who they are is bound to have more confidence than someone who is having to put on an act. People can see through a false persona quicker than you can say 'master of disguise'. So lose your insecurities and let the world see the real you

◊ **Dress like you mean it** – don't go overboard, dressing like you're the cabaret act on a cruise liner will not make people flock to your side, but make an effort. Wear a bright colour or dressed-up top with jeans, statement jewellery or a skirt if you're always in trousers. Anything that will make you feel a little bit 'party-ish'. Wearing something that attracts a compliment or two is also a good conversation starter, the first step to getting a group of happy people around you

◊ **Have a drink but don't get drunk** – well not until much later anyway. Knowing the recipe for a fabulous cocktail is always good and picking the people who look the most fun to help you make it is a sure-fire way of revving up the party atmosphere. But aim for a level of tipsiness similar to or less than the other partygoers. Being paralytic while all around are still sober won't win you any friends

IF THE GROUP OF PEOPLE
YOU ARE CHATTING TO IS
BORING, LEAVE THEM AND
FIND A LIVELIER CROWD.

◊ **Be interesting** – don't open the conversation with 'Hello, I work in finance'. Think around the subject and if you're really worried that your conversational skills are about as fascinating as watching paint dry, research a few topics before you get to the party. And don't forget, listening is part of conversation; don't get so carried away that you talk over the top of everyone

◊ **Try to lead and initiate** – the way not to be a wallflower is to actively make suggestions about what might add fun to the party. If the music isn't getting feet tapping, ask your host if you can change it. If the group of people you are chatting to is boring, leave them and find a livelier crowd

Handing round food or distributing more drink are great ways to break the ice and get involved in different conversations. Suggest a so-naff-it's-cool party game like pass the orange from under chin to chin. Major drinking forfeits ensue for the losing team.

Check your Breasts

Although 90% of breast lumps are harmless, the risk of cancer is always present so checking your breasts is vital. If you do spot a problem early on through regular breast examination, the chances of successfully treating it are high.

....

YOU SHOULD:
◊ Know what is normal for you
◊ Attend routine breast screening if over fifty
◊ Know what changes to look and feel for
◊ Report any changes without delay
◊ If over 50 attend routine breast screening

YOU SHOULD LOOK OUT FOR:
◊ Changes in outline, shape or size of the breast
◊ Lumps or thickening in the breast and nipple
◊ Any flaking skin or discharge from the nipple
◊ Any unusual pain and discomfort

There is a simple technique that you can use to check your breasts, which can easily be incorporated into your monthly routine.

WHEN TO EXAMINE YOUR BREASTS
Lots of women experience tenderness and lumpiness in the days leading up to the start of their periods, therefore the best time to examine your breasts is just after your period.

◊ Make sure you are relaxed and somewhere warm

◊ Undress from the waist up and stand in front of the mirror

◊ The appearance of your breast changes with the movement of your arms so start with them by your sides, then stretched up and finally with your hands placed on your hips

◊ With arms down, look at your breasts, turning side to side. Stretching up, look for anything unusual – not forgetting your nipples. Now press your hands on your hips until you feel your chest muscles tighten and look particularly for any skin changes or dimpling

◊ Now lie flat with your head on a pillow and raise your left shoulder slightly. Using your right hand for your left breast, press gently but firmly working in a spiral out from the nipple to the centre part of the breast. Keep your fingers together and use the flat part of your fingers, not the tips

◊ Now raise your left arm over your head and repeat the spiral check. Finish this side by feeling into your armpit as the breast actually extends right up into your armpit

◊ Now check your right breast with your left hand using the same technique

CURE A HANGOVER

Ideally we wouldn't get hangovers to start with. But that's unlikely. So a few ideas on how to stop the pounding head, sweating and general feeling of sickness and lethargy are always useful.

....

PRAIRIE OYSTER
Crack an egg into a glass without breaking the yolk and add salt, pepper and Worcestershire sauce. Down it in one. The raw egg contains an amino acid, which improves your liver function thus helping your body to clear out toxins.

A BIG BAG OF CRISPS
Sounds bonkers, but the salt cravings you have when you are hungover are due to dehydration. Alcohol is a diuretic that makes you urinate more than you should and lose valuable salts. Lots of water and a bag of crisps will go a long way to making you feel better.

A GINGER AND MELON SMOOTHIE

Ginger combats nausea while melons with orange flesh contain betacarotene, which is essential to help get rid of the bleary eyed syndrome. Remove the peel and pips from a large slice of ripe melon. Chop roughly. Grate fresh ginger to taste and whizz it all up in a blender until smooth. Drink.

VIRGIN MARY
Use a celery stalk to stir quarter of a teaspoon of grated horseradish, a twist of black pepper, a few drops of Tabasco sauce and half a teaspoon of

116

Worcestershire sauce into 200ml tomato juice. The tomatoes are full of bioflavonoids that will help clear out the toxins running riot in your system.

TAKE B VITAMINS

If one of your hangover symptoms is feeling really grouchy take some B vitamins. Alcohol saps the body of these vital vitamins, which are related to mood. Try a handful of Brazil nuts to help metabolise the booze as well as stabilise your nervous system.

BANANA MILKSHAKE

Liquidise a couple of bananas with milk and sweeten to taste. Alcohol makes you lose potassium, which is vital to keeping you body fluids balanced. A banana contains half your daily dose of potassium, plus Vitamin C, magnesium and natural sugars to help replenish your blood sugar levels – which will have been wiped out by excessive drinking.

Dance like a Diva

Are you a disco diva or do you have two left feet? There's no doubt about it, being able to impress on the dance floor is one of those life skills that many of us wish we had.

....

The advice below isn't going to help you learn to waltz or dance the tango – you'd have to learn the steps for that – but whether dancing on your own or with a partner there are a few things you might want to try.

Lose any self-consciousness
A couple of drinks may help but don't drink too much – you want to be memorable for your dancing not your drunken antics. Having a go at dancing is much more attractive than being a wallflower. Wait until the dance floor is full and a song you know and like is played – you'll be more likely to sing along and move naturally to the music.

Develop an instinct
While knowing and understanding the steps to a particular dance is obviously useful, developing an instinct for the dance or music is more important. Some people call it 'feel'. It is from this feel that you will find the correct timing for the music you are dancing to. Even if you don't know the steps to a dance, a good partner will be able to lead you if you can 'feel' the music. If you're dancing on your own your movements will fit the music making you appear a much better dancer than you actually are!

TIMING IS IMPORTANT

In dancing, there are two parts to timing. The first is the static beat that flows through an entire track and dictates when to move your feet. The other is the tempo of the music itself. It's the tempo that times the length of a dance step, the duration of a pause or how fast you should make a turn/spin and it's the tempo that tells you what move to do and when. Understanding how to move with the tempo will make you a better dancer. Let the music dictate what you should be doing.

THE BENEFITS OF SHAKING YOUR BOOTY

Maybe you're still not convinced to give it your all on the dance floor. But think of it this way: being a good dancer is like having a fabulous secret. You might not like how you look in a tight skirt or know that you'll never be a supermodel but once you get on the dance floor all that can melt away. Express yourself and let rip.

Drive a Sports Car

We all know that women are better drivers than men. But women driving sports cars often attract remarks from men such as 'Nice car, bet she never gets out of third gear' or 'great motor but I bet she chose it because the leather seats match the paintwork' and other hilarious one liners.

....

But if you know how to handle a sports car you can shock the little socks off them. Pulling a hand break turn or two and burning some rubber in the process will leave them clutching the bucket seats in admiration. Here's how to impress:

Know your vehicle

Knowledge is power and being able to tell a scornful man what brake horsepower your car is and how it handles in the wet will go a long way to convincing the world that driving a sports car is second nature to you. So find out – engine size, acceleration from 0–60mph, make, model right down to drag co-efficiency. Then understand the car's behaviour. Go on a track day at Silverstone to familiarise yourself with how it takes corners and the thrill of it when driving at speed. Showing confidence in your car is half the battle.

Accelerating

Your control over the car relies totally on the level of friction between the car and the road surface. And the most important single factor in

maintaining the level of friction is the way in which you drive the car. One of the factors that helps you control the friction is acceleration. To drive a sports car well you need to learn to accelerate smoothly and progressively. Acceleration force is limited by the power of the engine, your skill with accelerator, clutch and gears and the adhesion of the tyres to the road surface. If you accelerate too quickly you are likely to lose control of the car. Weight is shifted from the front to the rear of the car and the efficiency of the steering is reduced and could cause the car to skid. So avoid harsh acceleration and deceleration particularly in the lower gears. Use fifth gear as soon as your car is 'happy' with it.

Braking
Applying the brakes also requires skill so that you don't lose control of the car, particularly when

travelling at speed or taking a corner. Use your gears to slow down the car where possible, as this will allow you greater control over the car itself. Harsh breaking will result in weight moving from the rear to the front of the car, making the steering heavier to handle and reducing the adhesion of the rear tyres to the road surface. Again this can cause you to skid and lose control of the car. Instead be prepared to slow down early. Break gently and smoothly allowing a gradual reduction in speed, which gives you more time to assess the situation and make any necessary gear changes.

CORNERING

Cornering is vitally important in demonstrating your mastery at handling a sports car. It is influenced by the tyre and road surface adhesion, the efficiency of the suspension system and your own skill in steering.

Cornering at too high a speed can cause loss of control because the force of the car turning is pitted against the force of the tyre applied to the road. This means weight shifts to the wheels on the outside of a corner reducing the adhesion of the inside tyres on the road surface. Hence the lift you see when racing cars are going at great speed round a corner.

To remain in control and corner speedily but safely, maintain a constant speed when on bends and cornering. Try to minimise the need for sudden changes in speed and direction and power down, easing slightly off the accelerator before you reach the bend. Your approaching speed should be slow enough to allow you to drive around the bend accelerating gently as you do so.

Get a Butt
to Die for

**There isn't an easy answer to this one.
Unless you're born with one, getting a
great butt takes work. And that means
exercise I'm afraid.**

....

Squats are the time-honoured way of training your
gluteus maximus (butt). You can add resistance by
performing them while holding weights in your
hands. Varying the width of your feet will change
the emphasis of the exercise. The closer together
your feet are, the more your quads (front of the
thighs) will work. As you move your feet further
apart, you'll feel the exercise more in your hips and
butt. Get someone to check your form to be sure
you're doing the squats properly and your butt
muscles are doing the most work they can.

Lunges are another exercise that works the same
area. You can do them on the flat or try the step
machine at the gym. Another option is to use the
bottom step of your staircase. Build up the speed
and number of repetitions gradually.

Getting trim

Losing weight and shaping up generally will also
help highlight the shape of your butt and tone
you up. To kill two birds with one stone, try doing
cardiovascular exercises that recruit the leg muscles
to help shape your legs and also boost overall calorie
burning. Cycling, walking, in-line skating and
running all burn calories and tone leg muscles.

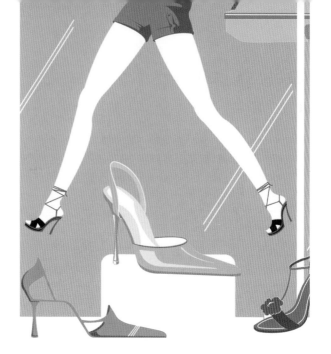

In-line skating is particularly good for working
your butt muscles.

Finishing touches

To keep your butt looking great you'll need to
exercise regularly but you'll get there. And when
the pounds fall off and the muscles firm, go for
some treatments to smooth the skin and improve
your circulation.

Finally go shopping. Buy snugly fitting jeans,
tight pencil skirts – basically anything that
emphasises your new asset. Then stand back and
wait for the reaction.

GET A MAN TO PAY FOR DRINKS

Now maybe you think this goes against sexual equality but hey, sometimes you might fancy a little bit of old-fashioned flirting and getting a guy to buy you a drink can be part of that ritual. Here's how to do it:

◊ Simplest method first – ask if he'd like to buy you a drink. He could say no, but if you've been eyeing each other up he'll more than likely say yes. Who wants to go out with a Scrooge anyway?

◊ Ask for a sip of his drink – run off the dance floor fanning your fevered brow. Would he be really kind and let you have a sip of his drink? Watch how quickly he offers to buy you one

◊ Accidentally lose your purse, say you gave your last pennies to a homeless man in the street or get indignant about the fact that the barman won't accept a card unless you spend a certain amount. Some kind chap will take pity on you

◊ Sidle up to him at the bar – while he's placing his order for drinks, give him a sensational smile and ask if he can add yours to the list and you'll pay him back. Chances are he'll say 'This one's on me'

◊ If all else fails – offer to buy him a drink. If he's any kind of man, he'll offer to buy you one back

Get him to propose

On the whole, women tend to be more marriage-minded than men. And on the whole, men tend to be more goal-directed than women. So when they come to making a decision about getting married they do it on more of a benefit-loss type system. For example, if I commit to marrying her, what do I gain and what do I lose? This may sound a little cold to us girls but the workings of the male brain are a mystery.

· ·

With this in mind try these tips to get him to propose to you:

Make him fully appreciate the benefits of being with you

Approach this one like a military campaign. Lay your plans and execute them efficiently, closing in on your target with skill and precision:

◊ Go out of your way to be funny, witty and charming and tell him that when you're both 85 you'll at least have something to talk about

◊ When you cook him a meal or do something for him, make him aware of the fact. Jokingly remark that you bet he's never been so well looked after. When he starts to realise he hasn't, you've got him

◊ After a night of great sex – where you've made sure he's really enjoying himself – remark how

you'd like to have sex like that for the rest of your life and then ask him how it was for him. This will get him thinking how great sex is with you and only you

LOOK TO THE PAST AND TALK ABOUT THE FUTURE

Reinforce why you're so good together subtly by talking about specific instances in your past. That time when you met his friends and you all got wildly drunk. Or when you had that fight about him not complimenting you on your outfit and then how quickly he got you out of said outfit when you made up. Or when you went on holiday together and lay on the beach looking at the stars.

Then start talking about what you're going to do next year on holiday or how you're looking forward to his best mate's birthday party next week. This will unconsciously suggest that you should be together in the future and get him thinking along serious commitment lines.

MAKE HIM AWARE OF YOUR INTEREST IN A LIFELONG COMMITMENT

Tell him that you can't imagine your future without him and how great it is that you share the same interests, values and common goals. This will have much more of an impression than you incessantly bombarding him with demands about marriage.

IF ALL ELSE FAILS...

Well, he just might not want to get married. But there's nothing to say you can't propose to him!

Win Any Argument

Now I'm sure your mother always told you it isn't nice to argue but sometimes it just can't be avoided. And what your mum didn't teach you, we can.

Of course, women win most arguments anyway don't they? But just to make sure you've got the technique down pat...

There's an art to arguing effectively: maintaining eye contact, avoiding empty threats, keeping your voice low and maintaining positive body language are some of the basics.

Staying in the room is helpful too – storming off will get you nowhere nor will having a kicking and screaming tantrum on the floor.

So to get your partner apologising with a bouquet of flowers, your colleague making you coffee for a month and your boss awarding you a surprise day off, here are some tips:

◊ Put forward your view. Ask the other person if they think your points are valid and allow them to save face by agreeing with all their minor points in a reasonable way. Stick to your main points throughout the argument, firmly but quietly repeating them if necessary

◊ Listen actively. Resist the urge to butt in and take up a neutral listening stance. Don't smirk or scowl

◊ Keep calm. Take regular deep breaths to help you keep your temper

◊ Have the last word. Let the other person rant and rave backing themselves into a corner. When they're stunned by your silence, put the boot in

◊ Back down gracefully. On the very few occasions you might be wrong, admit it. It may kill you at the time but could benefit you in the long term. If you admit your mistakes now and then your sparring partner will have to concede you're a reasonable person

◊ Pick your battles and walk away. If it turns into a slanging match you have to know that some things just aren't worth fighting about and walk away. Quit while you're ahead and before you irreparably damage your relationship. Protect yourself and maintain your dignity

Make a Killer
Cocktail

**This will teach you how to impress
people with your knowledge and
dexterity in the art of cocktail making.
Banish any notions of paper umbrellas
or saccharine margarita mix, you're
going to make the real thing.**

Cocktails are usually made with spirits as a base,
plus flavours, which can come from herbs, spices,
fruit juices or other spirits. Sophisticated cocktail
drinkers like their drinks strong – more spirit and
less flavouring.

By learning to make one of the classic cocktails
of all time, the Dry Martini, you will never fail to
impress people.

YOU WILL NEED:
2 or 3 ounces (60ml or 90ml) London dry gin
1 or 2 drops Noilly Prat, Chambery or Lillet dry
    vermouth
Lemon peel or olive

Put the gin and vermouth into a shaker and stir
well with three or four ice cubes. Pour into 4 ounce
(120ml) cocktail glasses. Twist a lemon peel over
the drink. Purists advise stopping at that and
forbid dropping the peel in the drink. Others, of
the old school, replace the peel with an olive. Serve
and enjoy.

Master
Self-Defence

In an ideal world we wouldn't need to know how to defend ourselves, let alone use self-defence. But there are a few things you can do, without the need to memorise lots of arm-locks and positions, to defend yourself should the need arise.

By law you have the right to defend yourself with 'reasonable force'.

The best thing you can do to an attacker is to inflict instant and intense pain so that he wishes he were somewhere else apart from attacking you.

To truly master self-defence you'll need to take classes with a qualified instructor. But there are many unprotected areas of an attacker's body that can be hurt quickly and easily. By attacking some of these areas you may be able to escape or create an opening to attack him again.

You won't have time to think about which of these approaches to take or where to attack him – just think nearest target, nearest weapon.

The pinch
This is one of your best weapons. A forefinger and thumb or a thumb and hard object like a pen can have the same effect as a pair of pliers. Twisting,

grasping and tearing can all be achieved with the simple pinch. Applied with enough force to fleshy parts of the body – nose, lips, Adam's Apple, testicle – you can cause a lot of pain.

Your thumb, especially if it has a sharp nail, is a very effective weapon. Pushed hard into the bone on the top or bottom of the eye socket will cause immediate and excruciating pain. Hooking your thumbs into the corners of the mouth or the nostrils and pulling should result in instant release. Or ram both thumbs into the nerve centres that lie at the hinge of the jaw in the recesses under the ear, or use them to put pressure on the nerve at the bottom of the nose. Both are very painful.

THE GRIP

Even if your grip isn't that strong, knowing where to use it is half the battle. Squeezing the 'love handles' area to the sides of the stomach below the ribs with all your might will cause shock and trauma to the system. The fleshy part of the back of the arm, inside the thigh and the ridge of fat and sinew that runs from under the arm to the nipple are all susceptible to hard squeezing and gripping them will result in huge pain. Don't forget squeezing and gripping the testicles as hard as you can.

BREAKING FINGERS

Sounds awful but it's one of the only areas of the body that you'll be able to break easily so that you can buy yourself some time to escape your attacker or disable him properly. The little finger is easiest to break – simply grab it and roll it backwards against the joint and as you feel it give way shake it like a dog with a bone. It will make your attacker think very carefully about whether or not to continue the assault.

1. Impair your attacker's vision – if he can't see, he can't find you to harm you.
2. Attack his respiratory system – if he can't breathe, he won't be capable of harming you.
3. Go for the vital organs – if he's in agony, he won't be thinking of harming you.
4. Impair his mobility – if he can't walk he can't catch you to harm you.

Plan a Hen Night

If you're ever asked to plan a hen night, you owe it to your best friend to do a good job. Follow the advice below and you'll have a night to remember:

Get the guest list right and set the date

Ask the hen who she wants to invite, get all contact details possible for each guest – name, email, home and mobile phone numbers. Advise your hen not to invite too many people, just close friends and not her entire department at work. Up to 10 is an ideal number and much easier to book for than parties of 20 or more.

Start planning at least three months in advance, as it is not always easy to get people to agree on a date. To avoid problems get two options from the hen and settle on the date the majority of people can make. Before you confirm it for definite, tell the hen who can attend on that date. If someone she really wants to come can't make it you may have to start again!

Activity, cost and suitability

You should consider all three of these areas when choosing what to do for the hen night. If possible set a budget with the hen – after all she knows what her friends are likely to be comfortable spending – and work to it accordingly. You want to minimise hassle and complaints early on. Then try to choose something to do that:

◊ Fits your budget
◊ You think the hen and her friends will enjoy
◊ Will involve all the potentially different groups
of friends
◊ Will be fun!

GAMES, TRICKS AND TIPS

Whether you are planning a weekend away, an
activity in the afternoon followed by dinner or
simply a meal then dancing in a club remember
these golden rules:
◊ Keep it simple
◊ The level of fun you can have with people you
don't know that well is often in direct proportion
to the level of activity you engage in i.e. don't just
sit around all afternoon so cliques form and
cousin Jane from Devon ends up sitting alone in
the corner
◊ Playing forfeit games, compiling a 'life album'
for the hen by getting everyone to provide photos
of her, asking people to bring along a present to
dress the hen add fun and involve everyone

WHAT NOT TO DO

◊ Force the hen to do anything she really doesn't
want to, e.g. wear fake breasts over her clothes
◊ Let her imitate lewd acts with anything she can
get her hands on
◊ Get her so paralytic she remembers nothing
◊ Hire a male stripper – please, no

Stay Sexy at
30, 40, 50, 60

As the old saying goes, age is a matter of mind –
if you don't mind it doesn't matter. This is the key
to staying sexy through life.

There are a few things that give sex appeal to any
woman, no matter what her age.

Self-confidence
Don't take assertiveness too far. Not being a
pushover, knowing how to have fun without
worrying what other people think about you and
taking control of your life all make you sexy.

Be a flirt
The great thing about flirting is that you can do it
at any age, with anyone. Keeping a mischievous
twinkle in your eye and knowing how to enjoy a
little wordplay will prompt a response from most
men – whether you're 39 or 69. And it will do
wonders for your self-esteem too.

Never say never
This doesn't mean being completely reckless and
putting yourself in serious danger. But taking a
risk now and again, having a bit of an adventure
and going with the flow all add to your sex
appeal. You'll feel exhilarated and life will be more
interesting too.

Less is more
You're not going to have smooth, youthful skin all
your life and your figure will go through a few
ups and downs too. But don't overcompensate by

going down the mutton-dressed-as-lamb route.
A well-tailored suit that hugs your curves or the
tantalising smell of your perfume is much sexier
than acres of wrinkly cleavage on display.

LAUGH
There's nothing sexy about a woman who never
laughs. Have fun. Your joie de vivre is the
ultimate in sex appeal. If you're having fun,
others will want to have fun with you. It's a
win-win situation.

ACKNOWLEDGEMENTS

With thanks to:
Breast Cancer Care
The Advanced Driver's Handbook
by Margaret Stacey, Kogan Page
How to Eat by Nigella Lawson, Chatto & Windus
Think, Act, Stay Safe with REACT Self-defence by
Steve Collins, Harper Collins

Index